Blackbeard and the Monster of the Deep

Written by Ciaran Murtagh

Illustrated by Nathan Aardvark

Collins

Introduction

Blackbeard the pirate was a real person, named Edward Teach. He lived between 1680 and 1728. There are many stories about Blackbeard; some are true and some are not. This one isn't. Or is it?

Chapter One

Blackbeard's ship, the *Queen Anne's Revenge*, sliced through the cold blue water of the Atlantic Ocean like a knife. I clung to the mast, my heart pounding with excitement. We had been chasing the *Mermaid's Pearl* along the east coast of America all morning and now we were ready to attack.

"Raise the skull and crossbones!" ordered Blackbeard.

I ran to the flagpole and pulled up the flag.

"Good work, Bill!" said Blackbeard. "We'll make a pirate of you yet!"

Blackbeard was the most feared pirate on the seven seas, but to his crew and me, he was like a father. He was quick with a joke, generous with his gold and a brave leader. Blackbeard had rescued me from an orphanage when I was six. Now, at the age of ten, I was his loyal cabin boy.

Blackbeard stood in the middle of the deck, his hair billowing and his silk coat trailing on the floor. Thick strings tied into his dark beard were soaked in oil and set on fire, and his eye sockets were blackened with soot. Sailors who saw this terrifying figure marching towards them usually gave up without a fight.

Blackbeard took his sword from his belt and held it high. "Fire!" he yelled, chopping the air with his blade.

Our cannons boomed and soon the air was thick with smoke. Blackbeard stood in the middle of the deck with his beard blazing, looking like a monster from beyond the grave. Cannonballs crashed into the side of the *Mermaid's Pearl*, splintering the wood.

Blackbeard grinned. He knew his pockets would soon be full of gold.

As the smoke cleared, Blackbeard leapt on to the rail of our ship.

"Come on, Bill!" he shouted. "What are you waiting for?"

My heart jumped for joy. Normally I stayed on board while the rest of the crew robbed the captured ship. This was the first time Blackbeard had asked me to join him. Was I a proper pirate at last?

Chapter Two

Blackbeard strode down the deck of the *Mermaid's Pearl*, his beard burning and his face grim. Men jumped out of his way as he passed. Blackbeard had been a pirate for twenty years and was wanted in as many countries. Thanks to his frightening looks and fearsome reputation, he never needed to hurt anyone when he attacked a ship.

Indeed, the ship's captain raised his arms in surrender straight away. Blackbeard watched as one of our crew tied him up.

"I am Blackbeard," he said to the captured captain. "We will take what we want and then set you free. No harm will come to you or your crew."

I noticed that the crew of the *Mermaid's Pearl* had lined up at the back of the ship. Out of the corner of my eye I saw something strange behind them. I was about to go and see what it was when Blackbeard threw open the doors of the hold and called me to join him.

"Let's see what treasures they are hiding!" said Blackbeard with a wink.

When my eyes got used to the darkness, I saw that the hold was full of gold and fine silks. Blackbeard was dragging a chest towards the stairs when a member of our crew, One-eyed Pete, appeared above us.

"Captain, you have to see this!" he said.

Quickly, Blackbeard bounded out of the hold. When I caught up, I could see that the captured sailors had been tied up and moved away from the back of the boat. Blackbeard and our pirate crew were now staring open-mouthed at whatever the sailors had tried to hide.

"What is it, Pete?" asked Blackbeard.

"I don't rightly know, captain," said One-eyed Pete.

As I watched, a massive tentacle rose up from behind the ship and smacked the deck.

"Get back, Bill!" ordered Blackbeard. "There's something deadly down there!"

Chapter Three

It took all of my courage to stare over the rail at what was lurking in the water. When I did, the biggest octopus I had ever seen stared back at me. It was trapped in a net that was tied to the *Mermaid's Pearl*.

"It's a monster!" cried Blackbeard, shaking his head in amazement. Ten of Blackbeard's strongest pirates dragged the net up alongside the rail. The octopus was as tall as three men and each of its tentacles was the length of half a ship.

"We found it in the Bahamas," explained the captured captain. "We were taking it back for scientists in Washington to study when you caught us."

"It's huge," I said, stepping forward for a closer look. The octopus watched me with its ink-black eyes. In a daze, I stretched out my hand to stroke its oily skin.

"Look out!" yelled Blackbeard.

But it was too late. The octopus let out an ear-piercing shriek, tore through the net and slithered towards me. I jumped out of the way as the monster's enormous tentacles lunged forward. In an instant, Blackbeard was at my side.

"Get behind me!" he shouted, taking out his sword.

Blackbeard stood between me and the octopus. I watched from behind a barrel as the brave pirate stared into its eyes.

"Pick on my cabin boy, would you?" he growled. "Why don't you try me for size?"

The octopus lashed out with a slimy tentacle and Blackbeard jumped aside. Then he spun on his heel and swiped with his sword, missing it by a centimetre. In an instant the monster was upon him. The octopus grabbed Blackbeard in a giant tentacle and began to squeeze. Blackbeard gasped for breath.

"No!" I shouted, rushing from my hiding place. But before I could get close, the octopus smashed through the ship's rail and slid down into the water, with Blackbeard clutched in its deadly grip. I ran to the side and stared into the sea, but Blackbeard and the octopus were gone.

Chapter Four

The waves rocked the ship as I stared into the depths of the ocean. Blackbeard's crew gathered behind me.

"He's dead," said one, shaking his head sadly.

"Eaten alive," agreed another.

I shook my head. I couldn't believe that Blackbeard was gone for good. What was worse, it was my fault. If I had stayed away from the giant octopus, Blackbeard wouldn't have needed to save me.

"I see something!" cried One-eyed Pete. He pointed into the water.

Underneath the waves I could make out the shape of Blackbeard wriggling in the grip of the octopus's tentacles. I should have known Blackbeard wouldn't go down without a fight!
His head broke through the waves and he gasped for air.

"Help!" he spluttered.

Blackbeard was dragged back below the waves before anyone had a chance to move.
I looked to my shipmates.

"Help him!" I shouted.

23

Our crew started to prepare a lifeboat, but by the time it would be ready Blackbeard would be drowned for sure! Without thinking, I snatched a sword from the floor of the deck and jumped overboard.

The icy water took my breath away, but as Blackbeard's head rose above the water again I took my chance.

Heaving the sword with all my strength I plunged it deep into the tentacle that was wrapped around Blackbeard's chest.

"Good boy, Bill!" gasped Blackbeard. "He's letting go!"

I lifted the sword again and swung as hard as I could. The blade chopped straight through the tentacle. Blackbeard was free!

I watched as the octopus sank into the sea, leaving behind one severed tentacle and Blackbeard bobbing on the surface.

The other pirates lowered the lifeboat and pulled us to safety.

"You saved my life, Bill," gulped Blackbeard with a wink. "We'll make a pirate of you yet!"

Chapter Five

Later that night, with the *Mermaid's Pearl* robbed of its cargo and its crew set free, Blackbeard summoned me to his cabin. Treasure covered every centimetre of the floor.

"Take your pick, Bill," said Blackbeard, pointing at the treasure. "You deserve a reward for saving me from the monster of the deep!"

I looked at the gold, emeralds and pearls that lay in piles around the room. I didn't need any of them. But lying under a table I spotted a golden spyglass. I picked it up and looked through its lens, as if ready to seek out our next adventure.

"Good choice," said Blackbeard with an approving nod. "It looks like we've made a pirate of you already!"

I slid the spyglass into my belt, and Blackbeard and I went to join the rest of the crew.

"Hoist the main sail!" ordered Blackbeard.

The crew rushed to their jobs and the *Queen Anne's Revenge* sailed towards a new adventure. The skull and crossbones fluttered from the flagpole and a brand new pirate stood proudly on her deck.

Becoming a pirate

happy   excited

nervous   brave   confident

Ideas for reading

Written by Gillian Howell
Primary Literacy Consultant

Learning objectives: *(word reading objectives correspond with Lime band; all other objectives correspond with Copper band)* continue to apply phonic knowledge and skills as the route to decode words until automatic decoding has become embedded and reading is fluent; drawing inferences such as inferring characters' feelings, thoughts and motives from their actions, and justifying inferences with evidence; predicting what might happen from details stated and implied

Curriculum links: Science, History

Interest words: generous, orphanage, reputation, treasures, tentacle, scientists, ear-piercing shriek, severed, hoist

Word count: 1,500

Resources: pens, paper, art materials, internet

Getting started

- Look at the cover and read the title. Explain that this book is about a pirate called Blackbeard. Ask the children if they've heard of Blackbeard. Ask them what they know about pirates.

- Discuss the cover illustration with the children. Ask them to describe how Blackbeard looks. What impression of Blackbeard does this give them? Who do they think the boy is in the picture?

- Read the back cover blurb together and ask them to speculate on what the terrible surprise might be, giving reasons for their answers.

Reading and responding

- Ask the children to read the story using a quiet voice. Pause at significant events, e.g. on p10 ask them if they think what Bill saw is important to the story. What do they think it might be?

- On p13, help children who need support with the pronunciation of *tentacle* to help them when they meet the word again in the story and ensure they understand what it means.

- Encourage the children to use an expressive tone when they read the dialogue and to respond to the verbs used in the reporting clauses, e.g. ordered, shouted, yelled, growled, spluttered, gasped.